# NORTHERN
# AND SOUTHERN SIGHTS
## LIVING IN Alaska AND Brazil



written by Jillian Powell
illustrated by Kathryn Prewett and Beccy Blake

## CONTENTS

# NORTH AND SOUTH

The Rodrigues family and the Jakson family both live on the American continent. The Jaksons live in the largest and most northerly state of the USA: Alaska. The Rodrigues family lives in the largest country in South America: Brazil.

## Alaska

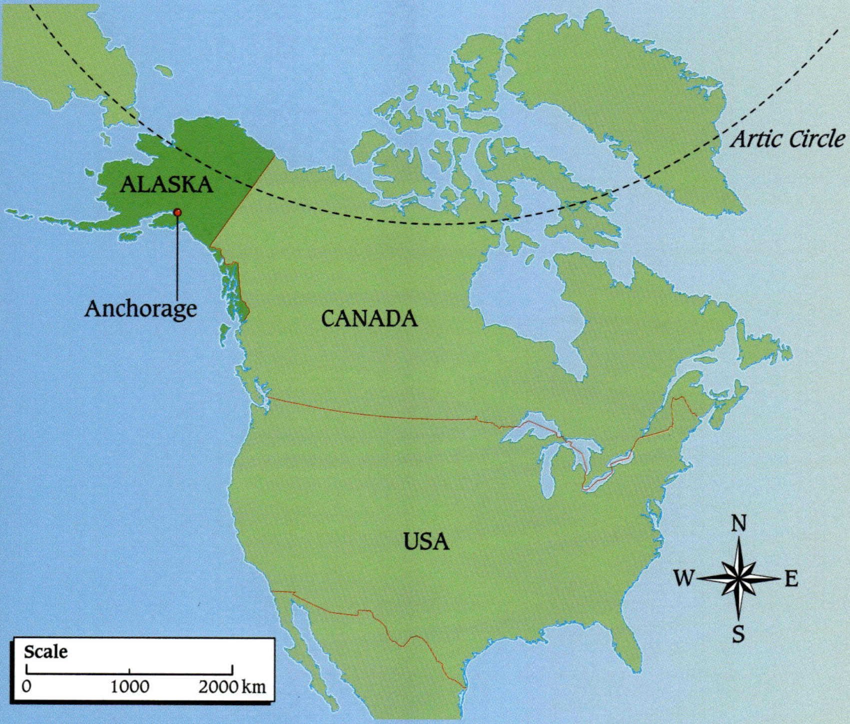


The Jakson family lives in Alaska, which is part of the USA. Alaska is separated from the other American states by Canada. Almost a third of Alaska lies north of the **Arctic Circle**. It has huge areas of wilderness and snow-covered mountains.

"There aren't many people in Alaska. We have almost three square kilometres each!"
**Tom Jakson**

**Arctic Circle** line of latitude which marks the southern border of the Arctic region

# Brazil

The Rodrigues family lives in Brazil, a huge country which covers nearly half the South American continent. Almost half of the country is covered with tropical rain forest.

"Brazil is so big that there are four time zones across the country."
**Antonio Rodrigues**

# Alaska

The Jakson family

The Jaksons are a family of four. Tom and Susan Jakson married 12 years ago. They met because they are both keen cyclists and belonged to a mountain biking club. They have two children. Caleb is 11 and Sarah is 9. The Jaksons moved to Chugiak-Eagle from Arkansas when Caleb was 4. They decided they wanted to live there after spending a holiday in the area.

# Brazil

The Rodrigues are a close family. Claudia and Antonio were childhood sweethearts in São Paulo. They married 13 years ago. They have four children: Jorge, who is 11, Gilberto, 9, Katia, 6, and Paulo who is nearly one year old.

The Rodrigues family

The Rodrigues live near grandparents, uncles and aunts, and cousins. The whole family sees each other all the time. When Antonio's family goes away on holiday, his parents look after their pet parrot Rico.

# Alaska

The Jaksons are not native Alaskans. Just 16 per cent of Alaskans are native peoples. The Jaksons' family came from states further south – what native Alaskans call "the Lower 48". (Alaska is the 49th state.)

The Jaksons, like most Alaskans, speak American English, although Inuit, Aleut and Indian native peoples in Alaska have their own languages and cultures.

A native Alaskan

# Brazil

The Rodrigues' great-grandparents came from Portugal in the early 1900s. Antonio would like to visit Portugal one day, and learn more about his family, who were farmers. Like all Brazilians, the Rodrigues speak Portuguese.

# Alaska

More than half of the people of Alaska live in the suburbs of Anchorage. The Jakson family lives in the suburb of Chugiak-Eagle. It has grown very quickly in the last 20 years. It is surrounded by thousands of acres of wilderness which Alaskans call bush.

The Chugach State Park

"Alaska is a special place to live. Native Alaskans call the rest of the world 'the Outside'."
**Susan Jakson**

**FACT**

Alaska is named after a word which means "great land" and it has also been called "The Last Frontier".

# Brazil

The Rodrigues live in São Paulo, the biggest city in South America. It is also the fastest growing city in Brazil. It is a modern city with skyscrapers and office blocks. On the outskirts are some of the largest shopping centres in South America. Beyond is farming and cattle ranching land.

The city of São Paulo

"We have a saying that people in São Paulo work while people in Rio de Janeiro play!"
**Claudia Rodrigues**

**FACT..................**

Brazil is named after Brazil wood, which is found in forests along the coast.

# Alaska

The Jaksons live in a log house. Most houses are built of wood which is then painted.

Every house has its own garden, which Americans call a yard. Most yards are open, with no fences between them.

The Jaksons burn oil and wood for heating so their house is warm in winter.

Caleb and Sarah have their own bedrooms and share a television and computer. Susan and Tom have fitted the house with modern machines like a dishwasher and a large freezer.

# Brazil

Today there are 19 million people living in São Paulo. The Rodrigues live in a new two-storey house. The Rodrigues' house is painted bright blue. It has shutters at the windows to keep out the hot sun. It is never very cold so the house has no central heating or carpets.

The door opens on to a street where no cars are allowed, so the children can play outside. There is a flat roof where the washing can be hung out to dry.

The three older children share a bedroom with bunk beds, and Paulo sleeps in a cot in his parents' room.

# Alaska

Break-up in Alaska

Susan's favourite season is spring. Alaskans call this time of year "break-up" because it is when the snow begins to melt and break away from rivers and lakes. The temperature rises to 4 °c.

In summer, the long days are warm and sunny. Then comes the **fall**, when the trees lose their leaves. Winter lasts a long time. The sun doesn't rise above the mountains for almost a month. But Caleb and Sarah love the winter because of all the snow. When Caleb was younger he once stuck his tongue to a snow shovel and it froze! There can be thick ice fogs, when fog leaves ice crystals on the trees.

**fall** autumn

# Brazil

The Rodrigues family likes the summer months best, even though it can rain a lot. They enjoy the summer because they love going to the beach, and having barbecues. The warmest months in São Paulo are from November to March, when temperatures rise to 28°c.

Because the city is so high (760 metres above sea level) it doesn't always feel warm. In winter it can be as cold as 3°c. The coldest months are June and July, when there are sometimes frosts and snow.

# Alaska

Like many families in Alaska, the Jaksons drive an all-terrain vehicle. These are important for getting around the countryside. The children like using their mountain bikes. There are lots of bike trails, which are used as ski trails in the winter months.

In the winter, they use a snowmobile. Motor vehicles are used instead of the traditional dog sleds pulled by huskies.

# Brazil

Like many Brazilian families, the Rodrigues family owns a car. Their car runs on petrol, but some people have cars that run on a fuel made from sugar cane.

There are so many cars in São Paulo that there are bad traffic jams and pollution. The air is often so dirty you can see a dull brown mist. Gilberto sometimes gets asthma which is made worse by the pollution.

Claudia uses the bus to go and meet her friends. The children sometimes go on the **Metro** with their dad to see football matches.

**Metro** underground train

# Alaska

Tom Jakson runs a construction business. He has to drive to Anchorage most days on a six-lane highway. Susan is a teacher at Chugiak High School.

The road from Chugiak-Eagle to Anchorage

The Jakson children go to Junior High School in Chugiak. A yellow school bus takes them to school. Each year in school is called a grade, and they have to take exams at the end of the year to move up a grade.

# Brazil

Claudia works part time as a nurse at the city Hospital in São Paulo. It is the largest hospital in South America.

The city Hospital in São Paulo

Antonio works at one of the car factories in the city.

Jorge, Gilberto and Katia go to school in São Paulo. Jorge and Gilberto study Portuguese, history, maths, science and art. Katia is still at primary school. Her classes finish before noon each day.

# Alaska

king salmon

Alaska is surrounded by two oceans and three seas so there are lots of fresh fish to eat. In the summer, the Jaksons fill their freezer with the local king salmon and red salmon. But the children enjoy American fast food like hamburgers too.

Susan goes shopping in the town of Eagle River, which is just a few kilometres away from Chugiak.

Hundreds of salmon swimming in a river

# Brazil

Claudia goes to supermarkets and also buys fresh foods from the street markets nearby.

A bowl of feijoada

The Rodrigues family eats lots of black beans and rice, sometimes served with a spicy meat stew.

The children's favourite foods are sausages and fried eggs.

# Alaska

Competitions are held in Alaska to catch moose and caribou.

In the autumn, Tom and his brother and friends sometimes go hunting for caribou and moose. They store the meat in the freezer to eat during the winter.

Blueberry syrup with pancakes.

"In the fall, we drive up to the **tundra** to pick wild blueberries. We make them into a blueberry soup and a syrup which we eat with pancakes in the winter."
**Sarah Jakson**

**tundra** Arctic region with no trees

# Brazil

"We drink a special kind of green tea called mate (pronounced mah-tay). It's quite bitter. The children prefer chocolate milk!"
**Antonio Rodrigues**

Mate is a type of green tea that is popular in Brazil.

On Sundays, the family likes to have a barbecue or "churrascou". They cook beef with salt on it. They have a small covered patio at the side of the house so they can have barbecues in the summer months even when it rains.

# Alaska

Like most Alaskans, the Jaksons love outdoor sports like skiing and snowshoeing. Dog-mushing is the official Alaskan state sport. Teams of husky dogs race against each other pulling sleds.

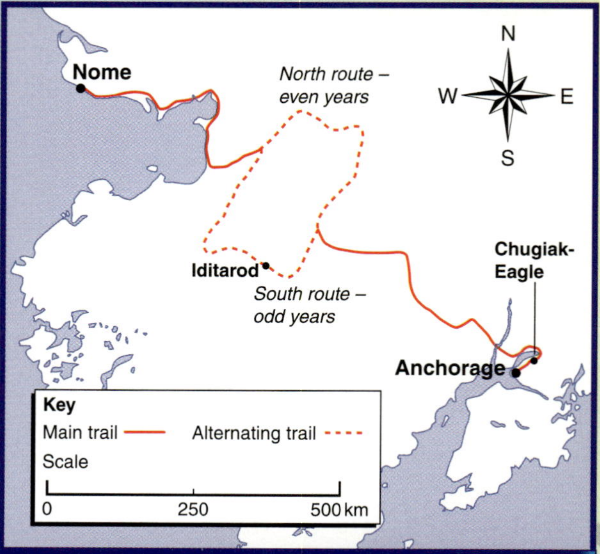


The route of the Iditarod Sled Dog Race.

The Jaksons enjoy mountain biking. Caleb and Sarah also enjoy sledging in winter and roller-blading in the summer.

# Brazil

Like most Brazilians, the Rodrigues family is mad about football. Brazil has over 20,000 soccer teams and is famous for its soccer stars. The world's largest football stadium is in Rio de Janeiro, but São Paulo has its own floodlit stadium that seats 80,000 people. Antonio takes the children to see special matches, but mostly they enjoy watching football on the television.

Rivaldo is one of Brazil's best players ever. He was FIFA World Footballer of the Year in 1999 when he was 27.

The Morumbi stadium in São Paulo seats 80,000 people.

In summer, the children like swimming and playing volleyball on the beach.

# Alaska

The Jakson family likes going to the **movies**, and sometimes they go out bowling.

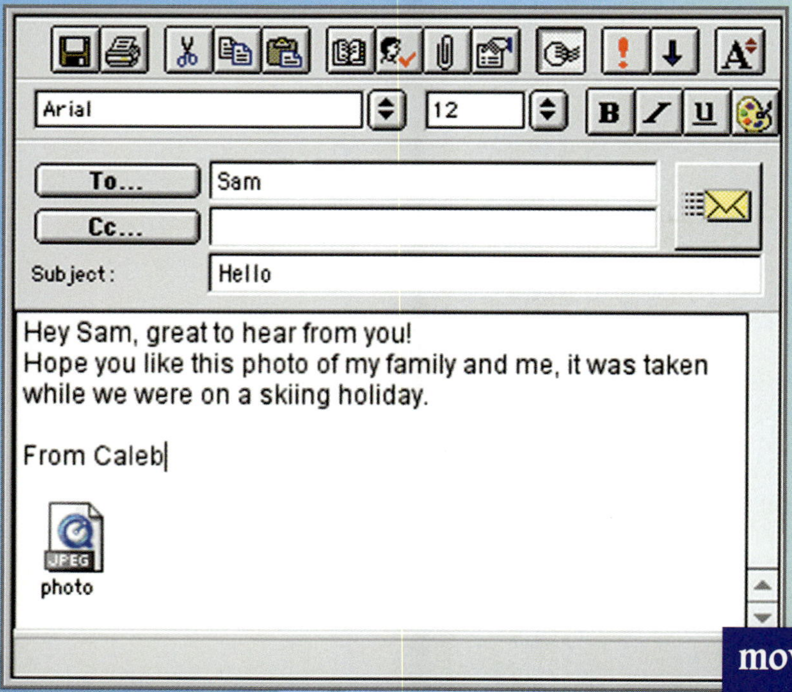


Eagle River has a six-screen movie **complex**, a bowling alley and ice skating rink.

All the family spend time using the computer. They have set up their own website, and send e-mails to friends all over the world.

**movies** films
**complex** multi-screen cinema

# Brazil

At home, the Rodrigues family likes watching television, especially football matches. Claudia likes watching the soaps, called "telenovelas". On hot evenings, Antonio sometimes sits outside and chats to neighbours.

The house is often busy with family or friends visiting. They like to watch football on the television together. There aren't many parks in São Paulo, so mostly the children play with their neighbours out in the street.

# Alaska

Every July, the Jakson family celebrates the Bear Paw Festival in Chugiak-Eagle. People come from all over the region. There is a family fun day, and a classic car show. It ends with a grand parade with carnival rides and games.

At midnight an 3rd July there are fireworks to celebrate Independence Day. Families bring picnics and blankets and come to celebrate under the **midnight sun**. Then on 4th July they have a parade.

The midnight sun is unique to the Arctic and the Antarctic.

"The best thing about watching the July 4th parade is you get to catch **candy** that they throw from the **floats**!" **Sarah Jakson**

**midnight sun** in the Arctic summer, there are days of continuous daylight when the sun never sets

**candy** sweets

**floats** decorated trucks

# Brazil

Every year, the Rodrigues family joins in the fun of carnival time in February and March. Carnival is celebrated all over Brazil. People dress up in colourful costumes, and sing and dance in the streets. There are fancy dress processions, and competitions for the best costumes and dancing.

Brazil is famous for its wonderful carnivals.

St John's Day on 24th June celebrates the corn harvest. The children dress up and paint their faces with burnt cork. People decorate the streets and have firework parties.

"There's a saying here that the noise of the fireworks on St John's Day will wake St John up from his sleep!"
**Claudia Rodrigues**

# Alaska

The Jakson family loves the outdoor life. Caleb has been learning fly fishing. When he was 9, his dad took him for a week rafting down the Alexander River. Last season they went to Tangle Lakes where they camped and fished for **grayling**. When he is older, Caleb wants to join the men on the **caribou** hunt in the fall.

**grayling** large fish belonging to the salmon family
**caribou** North American deer with large antlers

# Brazil

At weekends, the Rodrigues family likes to spend time on the beach. There are lots of people jogging, exercising and sunbathing there. There are boys selling soft drinks and fruit such as slices of watermelon. The children enjoy swimming and playing on the sand. Claudia and Antonio relax and read the local newspaper, *O Estado de São Paulo*.

a Capoeira demonstration

Sometimes, the family has a day out at the zoo, which is just half an hour from the city centre.

"Sometimes we get to watch 'Capoeira' on the beach. It's a cross between a fight, a dance and judo, all in one."
**Jorge Rodrigues**

# Alaska

The Jaksons love to see the "northern lights", the *aurora borealis*. They happen when gas in the atmosphere becomes charged with electric particles from the sun, and glows with colour.

> "However long you live here, you never get used to the northern lights."
> **Tom Jakson**

The best time to see them is in the spring or the autumn, and around the New Moon when the sky is dark. They look best when they are seen from a country lane, away from the city lights.

# Brazil

One of the Rodrigues' favourite things about living in Brazil is the football. The crowds wave flags and honk horns and beat drums. There are lots of families. It is very noisy and great fun.

"My favourite player for Brazil is Juninho Paulista. He was born in São Paulo in 1973. Dad watched him play for our team when they beat Milan in the world inter-club championships in 1993."
**Jorge Rodrigues**

# INDEX